I'M NO[T]

OVER

THE HILL

I'M SIMPLY TOO OLD TO CLIMB IT

Great Quotations Publishing Company

Written by Ron Cichowicz
Cover Illustration by Silvey Jex
Typesetting and Design by Julie Otlewis

© **1995** by Great Quotations Publishing Company

Published by Great Quotations Publishing Company
1967 Quincy Court
Glendale Heights, Illinois 60139

Printed in Hong Kong

Don't throw away the old
bucket until you know whether
the new one holds water.

- *SWEDISH PROVERB*

Hardening of the heart makes
you grow old faster than
hardening of the arteries.

You've been around the barn so many times, the cows recognize the sound of your footsteps.

When you're over the hill,
you tend to repeat yourself.

When you're over the hill,
you tend to repeat yourself.

You've caught yourself playing
connect the dots with
your liver spots.

You remember what life was like
before cable television,
microwave ovens,
car phones and Velcro.

You often ask youngsters to help
you remove a childproof cap.

You refer to anyone under the age of fifty as "young man" or "young lady."

When people praise you for
your leadership qualities,
it means you are starting to
resemble George Washington.

A woman never really loses the years she subtracts from her age — she simply adds them to another woman's.

But there's good news about baldness - it's a perfect cure for dandruff.

Old comedians never die.
They just gag a lot.

Time may be an excellent
healer. But as a beautician,
it's not so hot.

Then there was the old couple who got thrown out of the theater because he was talking too loud. It seems he was trying to whisper sweet nothings in her ear, but she had her hearing aid turned off.

Old age is when Mother Nature finally meets Father Time — and you're the one who winds up breathless.

You finally know your way around - but you don't feel like going.

Old age is that time when a man takes his teeth out more often than his wife.

A time when you complain
that your grown up children
don't visit enough.
But when they do, you can't
wait for them to leave.

The longer the cruise,
the older the passengers.

The older you get, the easier it is to resist temptation. But it's a lot harder to find any.

The older you get,
the better you use to be.

Definition of an old timer:
Someone who remembers when
you didn't have to thaw out the
food before you cooked it.

My grandfather always told me,
'Don't look after your money,
look after your health.'
One day I was looking after my
health, I found my money was
gone. My grandfather took it.

- JACKIE MASON

It's not that I'm afraid to die.
I just don't want to be there
when it happens.

- WOODY ALLEN

You're only as young as you feel.
When I get up in the morning,
I don't feel anything until noon.
By then it's time for my nap.

- BOB HOPE

Old fishermen never die.
They just smell that way.

Old accountants never die.
They just lose their balance.

Old lawyers never die.
They just lose their appeal.

Old age is a woman's hell.

- NINON de L'ENCLOS

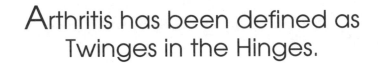

Arthritis has been defined as Twinges in the Hinges.

If your back aches before
you get out of bed,
you're getting old.

When I was young I use to say
good-natured things,
and nobody listened to me.
Now that I am old I say
ill-natured things and everybody
listens to me.

- SAMUEL ROGERS

The first hundred years
are the hardest.

- WILSON MIZNER

The oldest man alive today is reported to have celebrated his one hundred and thirty-ninth birthday. His case is regarded as a triumph of nature over medical knowledge.

- ANONYMOUS

When some fellers decide
to retire, nobody knows
the difference.

- KIN HUBBARD

Young men think old men are fools; but old men know that young men are fools.

- GEORGE CHAPMAN

Grandchildren don't make a man feel old; it's the knowledge that he's married to a grandmother.

- G. NORMAN COLLIE

Any archeologist is the best husband any woman can have; the older she gets, the more interested he is in her.

- AGATHA CHRISTIE

Retirement is the time when you never do all those things you said you wanted to do if you only had the time.

Life would be infinitely happier if
we could only be born at the
age of eighty and gradually
approach eighteen.

- MARK TWAIN

The older I grow the more I distrust the familiar doctrine that age brings wisdom.

- H.L. MENCKEN

When a man retires and time is no longer a matter of importance to him, his colleagues generally present him with a watch.

- R.C. SHERRIFF

Old age is when you first realize
other people's faults are no
greater than your own.

- EDGAR A. SHOAFF

First you forget names, then you forget faces, then you forget to pull your zipper up, then you forget to pull your zipper down.

- LEO ROSENBERG

I'm sixty-five and I guess that puts me in with the geriatrics, but if there were fifteen months in every year, I'd only be forty-eight.

- JAMES THURBER

You notice that the slowest driver
on the road is . . . you.

If I'd known I was going to live so long, I'd have taken better care of myself.

- LEON ELDRED

I refuse to admit I'm more than fifty-two even if that does make my sons illegitimate.

- LADY ASTOR

The only thing you seem to do in excess is produce stomach acid.

Life is one long process of
getting tired.

- *SAMUEL BUTLER*

Most of your favorite movies -
and all of your childhood photos
are in black and white.

When you brush your teeth,
you hold them in your hand.

When people ask you what President Carter was best known for, you say his little liver pills.

I use to burn and now I smoulder
That's how I know I'm
growing older.

- CHRISTOPHER MARLEY

You remember when a
refrigerator was an ice box . . .
you remember penny candy . . .
Or, you have trouble
remembering anything!

I always have trouble
remembering three things;
faces, names and — I can't
remember what the third thing is.

- FRED ALLEN

You know you're getting old
when the candles cost more
than the cake.

- BOB HOPE

Most of your favorite movie stars are either dead, haven't made a movie in years, or are doing commercials for denture adhesives.

You start paying attention to commercials for anything promising more regularity.

Your definition of safe sex is making out with anyone who doesn't have a pace-maker.

Your idea of a perfect gift is a
new set of bingo markers.

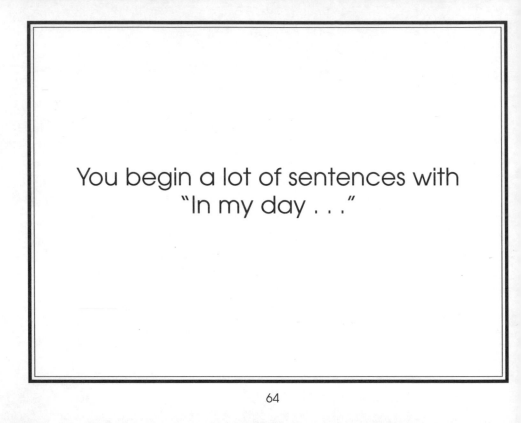

You begin a lot of sentences with
"In my day . . ."

The scent of your perfume or cologne is often overpowered by Ben-Gay.

When your body crackles,
it's not with excitement,
but arthritis; if it tingles, it's poor
circulation. And you no longer
burst with passion -
just irregularity.

When you tell your children they're going to put you in an early grave, and they say that's no longer possible.

You remember when a quarter
was a generous tip and not
an insult.

At an antique auction, a lot of items being sold are identical to those you're still using at home.

You buy clothes not because
they are fashionable,
but because they have a lot of
"give" and are easy to put on
and take off.

I'm still chasing pretty girls.
I don't remember what for,
but I'm still chasing them.

- JOE E. LOUIS

You're only young once,
and if you work at it right,
once is enough.

- JOE E. LOUIS

If God had to give a woman
wrinkles, he might at least
have put them on the
soles of her feet.

- NINON de L'ENCLOS

A man is only as old as the woman he feels.

- GROUCHO MARX

I'm not interested in age.
People who tell their
age are silly.
You're as old as you feel.

- ELIZABETH ARDEN

The best thing about getting old
is that all those things you
couldn't have when you were
young you no longer want.

- L.S. McCANDLES

What's the biggest problem with old age? There's just no future in it.

Old age is when you know all the answers but nobody asks you the questions.

Ve get too soon oldt and too late schmart.

- GERMAN PROVERB

I have discovered the secret
formula for a carefree old age:
ICR = FI
'If you can't recall it, forget it.'

- GOODMAN ACE

I am in the prime of senility.

- JOEL CHANDLER HARRIS

I'll never make the mistake of being seventy again.

- CASEY STENGEL

Whatever poet, orator or sage may say of it, old age is still old age.

- SINCLAIR LEWIS

As soon as a man acquires fairly
good sense, it is said that he
is an old fogy.

- ED HOWE

You've heard the three ages of man: youth, middle age and you're looking wonderful.

- FRANCIS JOSEPH CARDINAL SPELLMAN

Growing old isn't so bad when
you consider the alternative.

- MAURICE CHEVALIER

Now that gleam in his eye is merely the sun reflecting off his bifocals.

You've got to be fifty-nine years ole t'believe a feller is at his best at sixty.

- FRANK McKINNEY "KIN" HUBBARD

Old age is when the thing you
grow most in your garden
is tired.

A time when you quit dreaming that your son will become the president of a bank and just hope he won't try to rob one.

You're over the hill when it's no longer a thrill to get a window seat on an airplane, but it is to have one near the bathroom.

The brighter the colors a woman wears, the more she's beginning to fade.

If they ever decide to write a book about you, they'll call it "Withering Heights."

Bumper Sticker:
Don't bother to honk.
I won't hear it anyhow.

Old age is when you don't worry about how you'll feel when you get up in the morning. You worry about whether you'll get up.

In old age, you don't get feelings, only symptoms.

The names of all your favorite
soups begin with "Cream of . . ."

You can't stand on a street corner longer than five minutes before a boy scout tries to escort you across the street.

Your biggest social activity is
going to the funeral home.

When planning to visit friends,
you either have to call ahead to
make sure they're home,
or read the obits to make sure of
the visitation schedule.

You remember when a sanitation engineer was a garbageman, a flight attendant was a stewardess and an administrative assistant was a girl Friday.

When your grandchildren have to write an essay on ancient history, they ask you for an eye witness account.

When someone tells you they need a new set of plates, you wonder if they mean dishes or dentures.

Old age is a time of irony. For example, the more candles they add to the cake, the harder it is to blow them out.

You know you're getting old
when the candles on the cake
set off the smoke detector.

You start to buy industrial
strength Oil of Olay.

You buy Porcelana by
the gallon.

People no longer describe you
as "active", "virile" or "sexy."
No it's "mature," "distinguished"
or "senile."

When you look depressed,
people remind you to keep your
chins up.

The older you get, the farther
you had to walk to school . . .
and the deeper the snow you
had to walk through
to get there.

But it's nice to have something in common with your grandchildren - you both think their parents are idiots.

Your Superman days are over,
you act more like Mr. Magoo,
and look older than Mary Worth.

You get aches and pains
after just having thought
about exercise.

When you hear heavy breathing
in the phone, you don't know if
it's an obscene phone call,
or just an old friend.

You wish Domino's would develop a pizza with an oatmeal topping.

During a physical, you no longer worry about what your heart rate is, only that you have one.

You don't care if you have
"snow on the roof."
You just pray that your
foundation doesn't collapse.

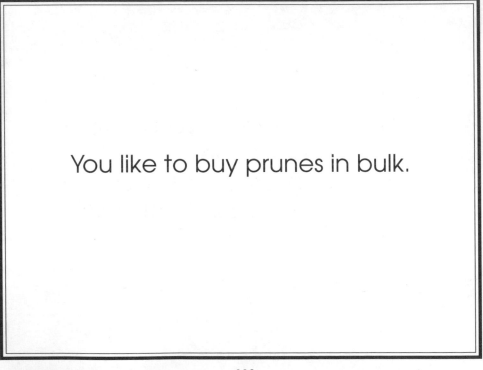

You like to buy prunes in bulk.

If McDonald's opened a
restaurant in your honor,
the arches would be falling.

You have a dart board at home
with Dick Clark's picture on it.

You keep an extra pair of glasses
to wear when looking for the
pair you always lose.

When you ask your doctor what foods you should avoid, he says, "What difference does it make at this point?"

When you overhear someone
say that the chassis is shot,
the body's falling apart and a
new paint job is needed,
you don't know if they're talking
about a car - or you.

You start advocating for bingo, bocci ball, canasta and shuffleboard to become Olympic sports.

Bumper Sticker:
I'm Over the Hill . . .
And on a Roll.

When you tell people you're like
a sports car. They say,
"Yeah, a Stutz Bearcat."

You've been known to enter a revolving door and come out the same side you went in.

When you see different speeds on a treadmill, you ask why there's no reverse.

You find that you're really
interested in watching
info-mercials on liposuction.

Beauticians have asked you to
sign a waiver . . .
or to bring in a specialist.

When you go shopping for a dress, you look for colors that will go well with blue hair.

When you walk into a drugstore, the pharmacist says, "So what will it be - the usual?"

People often address you as
"Granny," "Gramps" or "Pops."

Little kids ask you if you ever rode on a dinosaur.

Your barber says you're his favorite customer. Yeah - because he doesn't have much to sweep up after you leave.

Salespeople automatically give you a senior citizens discount.

People tend to speak louder
to you.

You always ask your grandchildren for help in working the microwave oven or VCR.

It's been a long time since anyone asked you if you're thinking about having more children.

You remember the days when couples consummated their marriage after the wedding ceremony.

When watching "Jeopardy!",
you get the most answers right in
categories like "The 1940s",
"Big Bands" and "World War II."

Your physician takes you off a
health maintenance program
and onto one for
"damage control."

Bumper Sticker:
"I'm not 65. I'm 35 with 30 years
of experience."

The only part of your body that's hard are your arteries.

Your broker only suggests
investments with a
short term yield.

You've considered building a Jacuzzi - but for health reasons.

The older the woman,
the redder the lipstick.
And the more she puts on.

You know you're getting old when people don't think you're lazy. They just think you're tired.

You get together with classmates to see who's falling apart.

Old soldiers never die. They just can't get into their uniforms.

You know you're over the hill
when a night out means
watching TV on the porch.

You know you're getting old when you reminisce about the good old days and nobody's qualified to challenge your memory.

The world is finally your oyster.
But you're too tired to crack
open the shell.

An old-timer is someone who can remember every detail of his life story, but forgets he just told you it yesterday.

Old age is when you go from looking good to looking well.

Remember:
Being over the hill is still better
than being under it.

Old age is when you don't go
out nearly as often as your
back does.

One of life's great mysteries is how someone can be over the hill, but can't remember ever being on top of it.

It's a time when it takes longer to rest than it does to get tired.

You know you're getting old when you can't get your motor started - but you have a lot of gas in the system.

Old age is a time when we enjoy
giving the advice to people that
we never followed as a youth.

You're afraid to "get down"
because you might not be able
to get back up again.

When the road you travel most
often is Memory Lane.

It's a time when your eagle eye has gone, and what's left of it is surrounded by crow's feet.

The hard way to stay young is to
eat right and exercise daily.
The easy way is to lie about
your age.

You know you're old when
you hear your favorite songs
on the elevator.

You're over the hill when you notice time flies - whether you're having fun or not.